A Tale of Two Husbands

and the Woman Who Wanted to Love Them

Simple truths for getting more out of your marriage (and your husband)

Angela Bart
&
Dr. Chris Bart

Angela Bart and Dr. Chris Bart
phone: (905) 515-6399
email: acbart@taleof2husbands.com

A Tale of Two Husbands and the Woman Who Wanted to Love Them
Angela Bart and Dr. Chris Bart

First Edition

ISBN 978-0-9938801-5-5

www.taleof2husbands.com

Special Thanks to:

Eleanor Bart, Karin Fleming, Anita Halfpenny, Becky Hicks, Julie Newman, Sarah Rogers and Steve Toffelmire.

Table of Contents

Foreword

Some of you might think us quite brave, my uncle and me. Here we are—a strategy professor and a teacher/writer—throwing our hats into a ring already bursting with countless weighty tomes penned by leading experts all promising to unveil the mysteries of the perfect marriage, or at least a better one! By now, women around the world have trekked all the way to Mars and Venus in search of the secrets to a fulfilling relationship. They've studied up on the care and feeding of husbands and on the finer points of mating in captivity. So what could possibly be missing from this plethora of marriage advice? Pearls of wisdom that only Chris and I can reveal? Well, as surprising as it sounds, we believe what's missing is some good old-fashioned Leadership Theory.

You see, Chris is the world's leading expert on organizational mission statements and how companies can use them effectively. For decades, he has been teaching corporate leaders around the world a few simple truths for getting almost anyone in their organizations to do what needs to be done. His approach helps people communicate clearly and ensures that everyone on the team gets what he or she needs to be productive and inspired in terms of accomplishing their organization's mission. What's amazing is that these same simple truths that Chris teaches to corporate leaders around the globe apply beyond the business world to almost any type of relationship. After all, a company is really just a group of people trying to coordinate their efforts for a common purpose. And isn't that what marriage is about too?

When I read Chris's first book, *A Tale of Two Employees and the Person Who Wanted to Lead Them*, I was struck immediately by how much his approach to helping businesses could apply to personal relationships, and marriages in particular. This was right around this time that my own marriage was faltering, so I was quite keen to try a fresh approach. After working through Chris's straight-forward process with my own husband, I became even more impressed with how powerful his ideas really were. They certainly altered the course of my life in many positive ways.

For years now, Chris and I have knocked around the idea of writing a book about marriage that was based on the advice he teaches to business leaders. And today, *A Tale of Two Husbands and the Woman Who Wanted to Love Them,* is the proud result of those many discussions. And yes, we know it sounds strange, a tale of *two* husbands, when no woman has (or would ever want) two husbands. But the story of Kamia, a young wife and mother living in a fictional polyandrous society is not meant to be taken literally. It's more of a light-hearted allegory designed to contrast how two different men might respond to the same approach a wife takes to create a more mutually satisfying marriage. Frustrated by what she perceives as her husbands' ongoing refusal to give her what she needs, Kamia seeks out the guidance of her wise old "Tuta" (her grandmother) who has been happily married to 6 husbands for many years. With Tuta's help, Kamia soon discovers how five simple questions have the power to turn a reluctant man into a supportive partner while revealing crucial truths about all his attitudes and values.

Even the most devoted husbands and wives can find themselves feeling like their marriage is not what they want—especially as life becomes complicated by obligations to children, jobs and extended families. The result can be loneliness and frustration for both spouses

13

with neither one feeling supported or understood. Unfortunately, that leaves thousands of decent, loving people unhappy in their marriages. But research has shown that happiness is mostly a factor of how much you feel in control of your own life. And that's how Chris's approach can really help women. By using the same communication strategies he has taught business leaders for years, women can overcome their exasperation with resistant husbands (or boyfriends) and gain a real sense of control over the quality of their marriages and the future of their families.

We hope you enjoy Kamia's story and the lessons it holds.

Angela

Chapter 1

The First Question:
Does he know *what* to do?

For Kamia, it was the best of times and it was the worst of times.

It was the best of times because she had just found out she was pregnant with her third child. Her two other children were 6 and 4 and growing more healthy and independent each day. Kamia helped run a successful family business that her grandmother had founded more than 40 years ago. She was smart and attractive and the envy of most other young women in her community—a small, little-known polyandrous society where women took more than one husband. At the age of 31, Kamia had already won the hearts of two husbands and was highly sought-after by other young men hoping to join her family. Kamia's husbands, Tom and Allen, were both charming and funny and both had good jobs that provided well for their family.

But, it was also the worst of times because despite how much Kamia wanted to love her husbands, they were driving her crazy! Her very traditional family was starting to pressure her to take on a third husband, but how could she even consider that right now? She was much too worried that both of her current marriages might actually fail.

And why?

Because for some reason neither Tom nor Allen was doing what Kamia needed them to do. Oh they covered the basics, but just barely. They worked hard at their jobs, did the dishes once in a while and played with the kids occasionally. But mostly, they seemed caught up with themselves and their own needs.

Tom was a successful electrician who loved to play tennis and was on the court every chance he got. When he wasn't playing tennis, it seemed like he was either watching it on television or searching the internet for the latest and greatest equipment or secrets to the perfect backhand. Kamia knew that Tom was an excellent tennis player and she admired the hard work he put into becoming the best he could be. It's just that it felt like he loved tennis more than he loved her and the kids.

On the other hand, Allen wasn't really into sports. His passion was business. He was head of sales at his company and he was obsessed with finding new and better ways to promote their products to clients and advance his career. Kamia had to admit that Allen was good at what he did and was an excellent provider, but he worked long hours and usually went into the office on weekends. It's not that she didn't appreciate all his effort, it just made her think that he didn't care about spending time with the family.

To Kamia, it just seemed like her husbands put their own needs and happiness ahead of everything else. They went out whenever they wanted, spent money whenever they wanted and expected sex all the time. They had no trouble just sitting back and relaxing with a beer after work. On the other hand, Kamia felt exhausted and overburdened. After working hard all day herself, she was usually the one left to deal with the kids and other domestic chores, as well as the constant goings-on in the extended family and community. *It seemed to Kamia that it all fell on her.* She believed that if she didn't worry and plan for all the eventualities of life, then no one else would.

Kamia was absolutely sure that her husbands had no idea how much work she put into simply problem-solving the details of their daily lives. But whenever she tried to talk to Allen or Tom, they brushed her off with either simplistic solutions or lines like "not now" or "can't you see I'm busy" while always reassuring her that everything would be fine. It upset Kamia that neither of her husbands really wanted to talk seriously about what was important to her.

All of this was made worse for Kamia because she always put the kids' needs and her husbands' needs ahead of her own. She felt like she always made sure everyone else was satisfied before she worried about her own happiness. From her point of view, *Kamia just didn't understand why Allen and Tom couldn't see how overburdened she was and how totally unfair their marriages had become.* Now, with their third child on the way, Kamia didn't know how she was going to do it. There was just no way she could keep up this pace much longer.

Despite her frustrations, Kamia knew married life wasn't all bad. She could definitely see the goodness in her husbands. After all, she did marry them both not that long ago. Tom and Allen were basically good guys and they could both be loving and kind when they wanted to be. Kamia believed her marriages could work and she desperately wanted to keep her family together, but she just didn't know how to deal with their problems. No matter what Kamia said or did, she was not getting the results she wanted. She was feeling overworked, under-appreciated and dismayed. Weren't these the two people who were supposed to be her partners in life? As far as Kamia was concerned, neither one of them was pulling his weight.

"I'm out of ideas," she sadly confessed one day to her best friend and unmarried cousin, Laya. "What am I going to do? I can't imagine being this unhappy for the rest of my life. But I also can't imagine allowing my marriages to fail."

Layla, who was younger and less experienced than Kamia, really had no substantial advice to give. "Wow, Kam, that really sucks! I have no idea what to tell you," Layla said as she gave her cousin a big hug. Then all of a sudden, the girl said something that would change Kamia's marriages forever.

"Hey, you know what you could do? You could ask Tuta for some advice. I mean, she has 6 husbands and she seems really happy. Maybe she could help."

Tuta. Of course, thought Kamia.

Kamia couldn't believe that she hadn't thought of asking her grandmother for help before now. Laya was right. Tuta had been married to 6 great men for many, many years and she always had a smile on her face. Tuta never complained about her husbands and Kamia thought that all her grandfathers seemed happy and satisfied.

That was it, then. With renewed hope and optimism, Kamia resolved to go and visit her grandmother the very next day.

***

When Kamia arrived at Tuta's house, she was greeted warmly by the wise old woman. Tuta liked Kamia. She saw her third granddaughter as a clever young woman with great potential. So much so in fact, that Tuta had recently put Kamia in charge of one of the smaller divisions in the family business. It made Tuta happy to think that she might play a role in helping Kamia succeed in life.

20

"So," asked Tuta. "What's the problem that you need to see me about? I would have thought that with your education, intelligence and tremendous talent that you wouldn't need any advice from an old woman like me. You appear to have everything, my darling. You're only 31 years old, everyone in the company speaks well of you and you have two strong, talented husbands and two beautiful children."

"And one on the way, Tuta," Kamia added softly.

"What joy indeed!" exclaimed the old woman. "Come and sit next to me, dear. You do make your Tuta proud. At this rate you will soon be telling me you're courting a third husband," Tuta added and then laughed out loud.

"Well that's just it Tuta. I know everyone thinks I should be adding a third husband very soon, but, well, I don't..." Kamia stuttered and then began to cry.

"What is it, my precious child? Surely it can't be that bad. You are a strong and determined woman who can conquer any of life's challenges," Tuta said encouragingly. "Please tell me what I can do to help," the grandmother pleaded as she gently rubbed Kamia's leg.

Kamia quickly pulled herself together and began to share her story. "Tuta, you taught me after Mama died that it is never wrong to seek out the opinion of others

21

when you have a problem that you're not sure how to solve. As a matter of fact, as a child you always impressed upon me the view that I should get as many opinions from wise women like yourself whenever I am faced with a challenge."

"I guess I did tell you that," Tuta said with a chuckle. "You've learned your lessons very well. But, enough of the flattery young lady. Tell me how I can help?"

Kamia began to explain her troubles to her grandmother. "You are right, Tuta. My life does look wonderful from the outside. I am becoming more and more involved and valuable to the business, and the kids are happy and healthy. It's just that I am worried that I won't be able to keep up with everything after the new baby is born."

"A new baby is a blessing, Kamia. This is just nerves talking," Tuta reassured her. "You and your husbands have done very well raising your first children. I am sure, once the baby is here everything will fall into..."

"No it won't Tuta!" interrupted an exasperated Kamia. "It won't all fall into place because I can't do it all by myself. Tom and Allen just don't help with anything! They only worry about themselves and their own happiness. They leave me to take care of everything at home while they go off and do whatever they want. They don't understand the stress I'm under with the kids and the business and organizing everything. The only time they ever really seem to show a deep interest in me is when it's bedtime and they compete for my attention and affection. I just feel so alone in my marriages. They never listen to me. I feel like I am the only one who cares about anything."

There was a short silence in the room and then Tuta took a deep breath and slowly said, "I see." Then, after a few more seconds of silence she looked directly at her granddaughter and asked, "But my dear, do they know *what* to do?"

"Do they know *what* to do?" a perplexed Kamia repeated. "Tom and Allen? Well, they certainly *should* know!" she exclaimed. "They watch me work day and night with the business, the house and the kids. They can see firsthand how unhappy and exhausted I am. If they don't, they're blind! Besides Tuta, they're grown men, they shouldn't need me to tell them what to do. I am their wife! They *should* know what I need from them!"

Tuta could see that Kamia was angry and hurt. "I see, my darling," the grandmother began. "You sound very convinced that your husbands already know what you

23

want them to do, but are simply not doing it. But are you sure Tom and Allen *really* know what you need them to do? My best advice would be for you to go home and ask them straight out if they really know what you want them to do. Just to be sure."

Struck by her grandmother's insistence on this question of whether or not the men really knew what she wanted them to do, Kamia sat up, furrowed her brow and waited a moment. She was confused, but she knew her wise Tuta must be getting at something important.

"Well, Tuta, I have complained so many times about how overwhelmed I am and how much work I have to do. In fact, we've had more than a few fights about it," said Kamia who was now clearly frustrated. "But if you think I need to ask them just to make sure—then I will Tuta." Kamia was very skeptical that this was going to lead anywhere helpful, but she did not want to disrespect her Tuta by dismissing her advice.

Kamia left her grandmother's house feeling disappointed. She had really hoped that Tuta would have been able to offer her a quick fix for her marriage problems, but now it seemed like she was back at square one. However, she did promise Tuta.

For a couple of days, Kamia said nothing. She wasn't even sure how to approach her husbands with this question that Tuta claimed was so important. She was definitely procrastinating hoping an opportunity to broach the topic would come up naturally. And indeed, it finally did.

One evening after Kamia had bathed the children and put them to bed, she walked into the kitchen she had cleaned up early to discover a new pile of dirty dishes left in the sink. From the baked-on cheese and salsa remnants, it was clear the men had made their favourite evening snack: nachos.

"Tom! Allen!" she shouted furiously. Upon hearing the desperate angry tone in Kamia's voice, both men hurried into the kitchen to see what was going on.

"I can't believe this!" she yelled at them. Kamia was fuming mad and the husbands could see it. Only they were both confused because as they looked around they couldn't tell what had happened that would cause such a crazy reaction in their wife.

Kamia couldn't believe the look of bewilderment that she saw on her husbands' faces. Could they not see what they had done? Their apparent confusion made her even more angry.

"Look at these dishes! Look!" She pointed to the sink in disgust. "I just finished cleaning the kitchen an hour ago and now there are more dirty dishes just left in the sink! What is wrong with the two of you?"

"Geez Kamia, it's just a couple of plates!" began Allen. He was clearly pissed off now. How could she be overreacting like this to a couple of plates in the sink?

"No Allen, it's not just a couple of plates. It's a couple cheese encrusted plates and two cheese encrusted forks! I just cleaned up the kitchen an hour ago and put the kids to bed, and now you expect me to scrub these plates for half an hour? It's bad enough you two never help me with anything, but you can't even clean up after yourselves?"

"Hold on Kamia," began Tom. "We just left those dishes in the sink five minutes ago. There's a game on TV right now. We were going to wash them up once it's over. Why can't you just relax. You know, every dish doesn't have to get cleaned 2 seconds after it's used."

"Oh really? I'm supposed to believe that at 11:30 at night after the game is over and you are both tired that you are going to come back to the kitchen to clean all this up? When I've never in my life seen either of you do that before? I am supposed to believe that?"

"Whatever!" shouted Allen in frustration. "You just can't let anything go. It's like you're looking for a fight all the time with us."

"He's right, you know," agreed Tom. "No matter what we do it's never right. What do you want from us anyway?"

"I want you to be responsible husbands and fathers. Stop acting like children and stop treating me like your maid!" yelled Kamia.

"Come on! I do not treat you like a maid!" insisted Allen. "I just emptied the dishwasher for you yesterday!"

"Yeah," continued Tom. "And I picked the kids up from soccer last night."

"Are you kidding me?!" Kamia yelled in disbelief. "You guys actually think that's helping out? Compared to all the things I do around here everyday that's nothing!"

"Oh my god, nothing ever makes you happy! It's always something. Even a couple of dishes in the sink set you off! What the hell do you want from us?!" exclaimed Allen as he stormed out of the kitchen.

Tom shook his head. "I have no idea what you want Kamia. I'm just guessing all the time. Nothing seems to satisfy you." He turned and walked out too.

Kamia looked into the sink at the cheesy plates and cutlery that were still sitting there unwashed. Finally, a light went on for her. They really don't know what to do. She did not understand how this was possible. After watching her do everything for months and months and hearing her complain all the time, somehow they still didn't know what she wanted them to do. Tuta was right. Suddenly Kamia knew she must return to her grandmother for more advice right away.

***

The next day, Kamia stopped by her grandmother's house after work. She told Tuta what had happened the night before. The old woman had no trouble seeing how shocked Kamia was that her husbands could not figure out what she needed from them.

"Tuta, I just don't get it. They watch me taking care of the kids all the time. They see me doing all the housework. I'm always complaining about how exhausted I am. How come they don't know what to do? It seems so obvious what they should be doing. So, why can't they figure this out on their own?"

"Kamia, you have to understand that as women, we are very intuitive," Tuta explained. "We don't need much information at all to infer what the people in our lives need. When it comes to our children, families and friends we can *see* what needs to be done and we just do it. This is our gift from nature. We are the caregivers, the nurturers. The goddesses did not bestow this same blessing on men."

"So what, then?" Kamia interrupted angrily. "Men just get to spend their whole lives completely self-absorbed and we women just have to take on all of the burdens of family life on our own?!"

Tuta could see the tears welling up in her granddaughter's eyes once again. "You are angry dear. I see that," she said. "But that is not what I am saying at all. Boys run around all day doing whatever they want seeking out power and pleasure for themselves. The spirit of the boy is in every man. They are the competitors and pursuers. These are their gifts. But, as women, we must teach the boy how to become a man, how to put the needs of others ahead of his own."

"Well that doesn't seem fair, Tuta," Kamia said indignantly. "Why is that burden on us?"

"Oh my dear!" chuckled the old woman. "Talk of fairness between men and women is the most direct route to unhappiness for all. The concept itself is quite subjective, anyway. Better to deal with the reality of the situation. Men simply need some help defining what their wives need from them."

"I guess you're right, Tuta. And I sure don't want to feel frustration and resentment anymore. I am tired of feeling that way. I just want marriages that feel like partnerships. I want to feel like my husbands care about my needs too."

"Then you must be *clear, precise and detailed* when you tell Tom and Allen what you want and need from them. But you must do this when you are not in conflict with them. During a time of peace, ask to speak with them and then *gently* and *lovingly* explain how you are feeling and what exactly–and I mean specifically and precisely–you need them to do."

"I still don't understand why I have to be so specific with them," complained Kamia. "When I say I need help, shouldn't they just be able to help me? When the baby cries and they are standing or sitting nearby, shouldn't they just want to go see why the baby cries and what they can do to help the poor child instead of running away or calling to me? When the laundry is piling up, shouldn't they just know to wash some of it?"

"You are thinking like a woman again, my dear," said Tuta. "Remember, your spirit is intuitive, you are able to observe someone in need and know how to ease their discomfort. You can even anticipate the needs of others before they are expressed. A man's spirit is not so empathetic and responsive. His potency and vigour are born of the fortitude in his heart. His strength and determination flow as easily as a woman's compassion and nurturing. Do you really desire to change that, Kamia? To make the tiger less powerful or the oak tree less resistant to the gale?"

"Well no, of course not, Tuta." Kamia conceded. "I love and admire the strength and beauty of the male spirit. I just wish..."

The grandmother sternly interrupted. "There is no room for *wishing* in marriage, young woman. Wishing is for the frail and inept. My granddaughter is a powerful spirit perfectly able to influence the outcome of her own life without relying on wishes."

"Yes, of course, Tuta."

Tuta went on, more calmly now. "Although your husbands might lack an intuitive ability to meet your needs, this does not release them from their duty to become supportive partners in your family. Despite their limitations, a man who truly values his marriage really does have a deep desire to please his wife."

"Well it sure doesn't seem like that most of the time."

"You must trust me dear. There can be no doubt that a happy, satisfied wife is a man's greatest joy while a dissatisfied wife is his greatest frustration," the wise woman extolled. "Kamia, I know you well enough to know that you do not wish to be anyone's greatest frustration. This is why you have put up with your husbands' boyish ways. But you must now do your part to help Tom and Allen understand exactly what they–as grown men–can do to make you happy. You cannot assume they will figure it out through observation alone. If they love you and value your marriage, as I expect they do, they will be enthusiastic participants in making it better. Just remember to be *clear, specific, and detailed* when you tell them what you need."

"OK Tuta, I'll do that." said Kamia with some hesitation.

"You see my dear," Tuta went on. "It is one thing for someone to hear a message, but they must also understand it. They must have enough information and detail to be able to visualize what you are asking for.

They really need to be able to *see* themselves doing the things you want them to do."

"They need to *see* themselves doing it," repeated Kamia nodding.

"It is only when people can *see* what it is that they are supposed to do that they will really be able to say that *they know what to do*."

"I think I am beginning to understand...uh...I mean *see*," Kamia chuckled.

"Alright then, now tell me exactly what you are going to ask for," insisted Tuta.

"Right now?" asked Kamia.

"Yes, right now dear. I want to hear you explain what you need from your husbands to make you happy. I want to hear you be clear, specific and detailed."

"OK. Let me see, now," Kamia began. "I guess I want them to help more with the chores and with the kids. And I want them to spend more time with me and the family in a way that really shows they value us. Oh, and I also want them to listen more attentively when I need to talk about what's going on in my life. You know, when I have a problem at work, or with our extended families."

Tuta looked a bit dissatisfied with her granddaughter's answer. "That still sounds very vague to me, dear. Remember, you want Tom and Allen to really see in their minds exactly what you want them to do. Try again, but this time be more specific. In what way do you want Tom and Allen to help with the children? Which chores would you want them to do? When and where should you spend time together as a couple? As a family? And tell them exactly what you need them to do to be better listeners."

"I know that's a lot to think about, Kamia," declared Tuta. "Maybe you should first try writing your thoughts down on paper." Tuta stood up and got a pen and a piece of paper out of her desk drawer and handed them to her granddaughter. Kamia began writing. As she wrote, she spoke her thoughts out loud for Tuta to hear.

"OK, let me think. It would be great if they could give the kids their bath each night and then read them a story and put them to bed. If I knew that was going to happen everyday, then I could plan on getting some work done during that time."

Tuta smiled approvingly. "Well now, that is much more detailed."

"And as for helping with chores around the house," Kamia continued. "Since I prepare dinner, it makes sense that they should clean up the kitchen and make sure the dishes are done. Also, I think they should do some laundry on the weekend. And not just run the washer, but dry the clothes and put them away." Kamia was writing furiously at this point. She seemed to be getting the hang of it now. "Oh yes, and I also want them to spend more time with us on the weekend. Maybe we could pick two or three hours on Sunday afternoon to designate as family time and then plan simple things to do like take a walk or play a game or something."

"Very good dear. I think there was just one other thing you wanted, wasn't there?" asked Tuta.

Kamia looked up from her paper for a moment and then answered. "Right, it was listening when I talk. I mean *really* listening. Whenever I am upset about a problem at work or about something my sister did, they always just want to reassure me that it'll all be OK. They don't get that I just want them to listen. Really, just listen and let me talk. It's like they're afraid of my emotions or something..."

"OK Kamia. That might be a little bit too much detail," Tuta said smiling. "Try to keep your request specific. Men often think you want them to solve your problems. It makes them feel strong. So why not simply tell them that when you are upset, you just want them to listen to what you have to say and that you are not looking for solutions. That you'd really just like a sympathetic ear that lets you know they understand how you must be feeling."

"Yes! That's it," agreed Kamia. "I just want them to listen and tell me they understand how I feel." Kamia started to write again.

"Now you're getting the idea, my dear," Tuta said with encouragement. "You will find the more clear, specific and detailed you are, the better a response you will get from your husbands. If they can see themselves doing what you want, then they will be better equipped for success."

"OK, but when I look at this list, it seems like I'm being pretty bossy and demanding. I'm worried they won't take that well at all. I mean, you know how men hate to be told what to do."

"Indeed I do my dear!" exclaimed Tuta. "As a young wife, I certainly stumbled around that problem more than once or twice," she chuckled. "Your concern about this potential difficulty demonstrates your intelligence and wisdom, sweet girl. Allow an old woman to tell you what she has learned over the decades about making requests of men."

Kamia sat up and leaned in towards Tuta awaiting the wise woman's next revelation.

Tuta continued. "It is very important to understand that because men so desire to please women, they take criticism as a sign of personal failure which causes them to be extremely defensive when you express dissatisfaction with them. This is why you must try to avoid the language of failure when you are making requests of your husbands. It is best to begin with a *statement of admiration* and then maintain a very respectful loving tone when you discuss your needs."

"A statement of admiration?" asked Kamia. "I don't even know what that means."

"Let me tell you something, my dear girl," said Tuta. "Men seek out and value admiration more than anything else, more than love, even more than money and power. And admiration from women is particularly valued. For a man to be in a loving, receptive place emotionally, he must feel that his wife admires who he is and what he has to offer her and their family. So you must always *precede* a complaint with a statement of admiration, that is if you wish for Tom and Allen to be in the right state of mind to embrace your requests."

"OK, so I should say something about them that I admire," Kamia said as though thinking aloud. "Well, I do admire how funny Tom is. He has a tremendous sense of humour and can make me and the children laugh the best. Allen on the other hand is a tireless competitor who manages to accomplish so much with apparent ease at such a demanding job."

"That's good," said Tuta. "So then tell Tom how much you value the way his light-heartedness cheers you up after a long day which makes it easier for you to be patient with the children. And tell Allen what comfort it brings you to know that he is such a generous and reliable provider. Don't you think they would both be pleased to hear those things?"

"Oh yes, I'm sure they would, Tuta."

"What's important," continued Tuta, "is that you are sincere and that you speak to and acknowledge the contributions they are already making to enhance their marriage to you. Remember, if they are like most normal men, they really do want to please you as their wife—but be warned, like most normal men, they are also very sensitive to your criticism. They need to know they are valued and so you need to make sure that they feel appreciated for what they are already doing well before you ask them for more."

"OK Tuta. I think I get it. So then what?" Kamia was very clearly excited by the prospect of using her grandmother's advice with her husbands.

Tuta continued with her instruction. "Next, you should tell them that you know they want you to be happy. It will ease their minds to hear this. Just don't forget to be clear, precise and detailed. Oh, and respectful. Always be respectful of the delicate male ego."

Kamia couldn't help but laugh out loud.

"Why are you laughing granddaughter? A man's ego is a serious thing, no laughing matter at all."

"OK sure Tuta. But isn't that kind of silly? I mean shouldn't a grown man be able to hear some reasonable criticism from me without getting his feelings hurt?"

"*Should* is a very unhelpful word, Kamia," Tuta scolded. "What you think a man *should or shouldn't* be able to do is of little importance here. It is a dangerous distraction. As wives, we must be concerned only with the truth, with the reality of the male spirit. A strong, robust ego makes a man powerful and confident. This in turn makes him far more capable of being a loving husband and of meeting your needs as a wife. A smart woman nurtures her husband's ego as she understands it is the source of his virility and devotion to her."

"Wow. That's a lot to take in, Tuta," declared Kamia with a sigh. "I think I need to take more notes." Kamia picked up her pen and paper again. She began taking notes as she summarized her grandmother's lesson out loud.

"So what you are saying Tuta, is that I need to approach Tom and Allen gently using respectful language that honours their masculine spirit. When I talk to them, I should begin by expressing some sincere appreciation for their positive qualities and contributions to our marriage. And then, when I tell them what I need, I must be clear, precise and detailed so they know exactly what I want them to do. I need to make sure they understand what I want in a way that allows them to see it in their heads."

"You are a good listener, Kamia," said Tuta with a smile of approval. "Just remember that you don't want to have these discussions with your husbands when you're angry or upset. Pick a time when there is no conflict between you to begin a dialogue with them. But don't wait too long. Have your discussions with them soon while our conversation today is still fresh in your mind."

"Yes Tuta. I will do it this week and I will come back to see you shortly to let you know how it went."

"I would like that very much my dear."

The two women embraced and Kamia set off for home with her notes tucked safely in her pocket.

***

Kamia spent a couple of days thinking about how she would approach her husbands using Tuta's advice and suggestions. She reviewed her lists and developed a plan. To keep things simple, she decided only to discuss issues related to everyday life and chores with Tom and Allen first. She would save the stuff about listening and Sunday family time for later. Let's see how it goes with just getting some help from them on a regular basis, she thought.

Friday night after the kids were in bed and everyone seemed in a good mood, Kamia asked both the men to join her in the living room to discuss some family matters. They came in and sat down looking a bit nervous. As Tuta suggested, Kamia began with some positives.

"I am so lucky to have such loving, devoted and sexy men as my husbands," she began. "I wish there was more I could do to show my love and appreciation for you both. I know that when the evening comes I am often so tired that I can get cranky sometimes. And I know you would both like more attention in the bedroom."

Both men seemed to relax hearing Kamia's words. They were obviously relieved that she did not call them together to scold them about something they weren't doing right as she has done most times in the past. Tom and Allen were also pleased to hear Kamia speak so positively about them and to acknowledge that she wasn't always the perfect wife. They certainly were not going to argue with her about wishing there could be more sex.

Tom was the first of the husbands to speak. "Hey babe, that's OK. We know how busy you are with work and the kids. Maybe there is more that Allen and I can do to help out around here." Kamia chuckled inside thinking how funny it was that Tom brought this to her as a new idea even though she had asked for help so many times before. She felt some irritation building inside her, but she quickly squashed it in favour of keeping things going in a positive direction.

"Sure, yeah. We could help out a bit more," added Allen who also was acting like this was the first time he'd ever thought about it.

"Well, I know you guys are busy too," said Kamia. "What with work and your other commitments. But it would be awesome if there was any way you could pitch in a bit more." Kamia was getting excited now at how well this was going but she tried to contain her glee and keep her voice calm and neutral. "It would be great if I wasn't so tired at night." In her mind she thought it would be a good idea to allude to the sex again hoping it would encourage the men's enthusiasm for helping out.

"What kind of stuff were you thinking of?" asked Tom. Allen looked a bit skeptical, but somewhat interested in what Kamia would propose.

"Well," she began. "What if you two shared the job of cleaning up the kitchen after dinner and getting the kids ready for bed?" She then gingerly added: "And maybe some laundry on the weekend?"

The two men looked at each other quizzically. This very general request sounded OK with them, so they both nodded in agreement. Kamia was quick to interpret this as her chance to get specific about what she wanted them to do.

"OK," Kamia said with a quick sigh of relief. "So after dinner, you two will load the dishwasher, and clean up the kitchen while I do some work in the office. Does that sound OK to you both?"

"OK sure," said Tom.

"Yeah, I guess so," said Allen with a bit of hesitation.

Things seemed to be going OK, so Kamia went on. "And then at 7:00 I would love it if you would bathe the kids, read them a story and put them to bed, OK?"

"Yeah, I think we can do that too," began Tom. "It might even be fun hanging out with the kids a bit more."

"Yeah maybe," said Allen, "but I might not be able to do all this every night." Kamia could hear some reluctance in Allen's voice. "I mean what if I work late or if I have to get a sales report finished? There has to be some flexibility here. I don't want you to bite my head off if I can't be home *every* single night for all this."

"Of course, Allen," Kamia said, trying not to reveal how irritated she was at his attitude. "Everyone will have times when they can't be home. And when that happens, we will all pitch in to help. I am just talking about the nights when you are home, OK?"

"Yeah, man," Tom interjected. "You and I will figure it out. Sometimes I have a late tennis game too. Let's give it a try and do the best we can."

"Alright. Fine. We'll give it a try," said Allen unenthusiastically. He then got up to leave. "Sorry, I now have to get some work done," he mumbled as he headed to his office.

"Don't worry," said Tom reassuringly to Kamia. "He'll come around. I know how much he wants to make you happy. We both do. The two of us will figure this out and make sure everything gets done."

"Thanks, baby. I appreciate it."

Tom also got up and gave Kamia a kiss on the lips. "You coming to bed now?" he asked as he got up to leave.

"Yes, in a minute," she said. Then she called out to him gently. "Tom?"

"Yes, babe?"

"You understand what I am asking for, right? I mean you can really *see* yourself doing these things?"

"Yeah. I can *see* myself doing it all," he chuckled. "Now come to bed with me." He smiled sexily and took her hand as they left the room together.

Chapter 2

The Second Question:
Does he know *how* to do it?

Over the next few weeks, both Allen and Tom did try to help out a lot more. The laundry was not piling up like it used to and the after-dinner routine was definitely improving somewhat. Interestingly, Tom seemed to lead the charge most nights being the first to get up from the dinner table to start cleaning up. Allen reluctantly pitched in, but it was clear that he was not entirely happy about the new routines. As Kamia had promised herself, she headed into her office after dinner to get some work done while her husbands took care of dishes and bedtimes.

However, it wasn't long before Kamia grew frustrated again. While both Tom and Allen were both doing more than before, she thought they were being pretty sloppy about their jobs. Plus, they would often "forget" about what needed to be done. A couple of different times, Kamia actually had to break up a bickering match between the fathers and the children during bath time. And lately, the kids started complaining that the dads would sometimes try to put them to bed without a bedtime story.

Even more concerning was the fact that Kamia was noticing that both husbands were becoming a bit cranky with her, especially when she would point out the wet towels on the floor in the bathroom after the kids' baths or the sticky kitchen counters or some unfolded laundry. Also, she was starting to get pretty angry that she was having to remind them of their responsibilities a lot of the time. Tom was somewhat apologetic when he forgot to get something done, but Allen was down-right defensive–even offended–when she tried to remind him. In order to avoid their bad moods, Kamia often found it easier sometimes just to keep quiet and finish up the men's work on her own. It just seemed easier to do it herself rather than run around afterwards fixing everything they had done wrong or missed.

Things were deteriorating fast and Kamia knew it. She also knew Tuta would not be happy with the results she was getting. Maybe the girl had missed something in the grandmother's advice. Perhaps it was time for another visit.

***

At Kamia's invitation, Tuta came over for tea one afternoon when the husbands were both out of the house. As the kids played in the backyard, Kamia began sharing her frustrations with her grandmother.

"I just don't know what I'm doing wrong, Tuta," an exasperated Kamia announced. "It was all going so well at first. Tom and Allen appeared very clear on what it was I wanted them to do and they were both keen at the beginning. But now, they both seem to resent the fact that they have to help out. I have to remind them all the time to do their jobs. Plus, when they are home they don't even do things right!"

"I see," said Tuta pensively. "And you are sure *they know exactly what you want them to do?*"

"Oh yes. We had a long talk about it and they agreed to everything. I even made sure they could 'see' what I was asking them to do."

"Well," sighed Tuta. There was a brief pause and moment of silence before the grandmother continued. "I think I'd like to say hello to my beautiful great-grandchildren. Would you make me a cup of my special lemon ginger iced tea while I visit with them in the backyard for a few minutes?"

Kamia was surprised at how quickly her grandmother changed the subject and how she seemed to abandon the conversation they were having about her problems. The girl was becoming worried that her grandmother had grown tired of her requests for advice and was no longer interested in helping her sort them out. What if Tuta was giving up on her? Despite Kamia's concerns, she loved and respected her grandmother, so she agreed to make the tea and allow Tuta some time with the kids.

"OK Tuta," Kamia said hesitantly. "They will be pleased to see you."

Tuta headed outside and Kamia got up to start making the tea. Her grandmother's lemon-ginger iced tea was a family favourite. Kamia used to ask for it as a child every time she went to visit Tuta. It was sweet and tangy and wonderfully refreshing. As she began assembling the ingredients she needed for the tea she found herself struggling to remember everything she needed. This was a recipe she had seen Tuta make many times, but for some reason, she wasn't sure exactly how to do it herself. She pulled some green tea from the cupboard and a lemon from the fridge. There was a piece of ginger ready to grate sitting on the counter. But she knew there was more to it than that. Her grandmother added some spices to the tea as well. Cinnamon, maybe? She put the kettle on to boil and checked the freezer for ice cubes. Then she became more concerned. How much tea should she use? How long should it steep? As time passed, she began to panic. She new Tuta would be back soon and she was still struggling just to get the tea started.

She was already worried about looking bad because of her marriage problems and now it seemed she couldn't even make a simple cup of tea. There was no doubt she was becoming quite frazzled.

A few moments later, Tuta walked back in from the yard.

"Oh my dear, the children are so charming!" she began. "You and your husbands should be very proud of your budding family. Do you have my tea ready?"

Kamia stumbled to find the words to explain herself. "Not just yet Tuta. The kettle has boiled and the ginger is cut, but I can't seem to remember how much tea to add, and how long it should steep. And did you add cinnamon? Or was it nutmeg? I don't know what's wrong with me, I just can't seem to figure it all out. You must think I'm a bumbling idiot. I can't make my marriages work and I can't remember how to make a simple cup of tea!" exclaimed Kamia in frustration.

"Well, dear. I'm not surprised you are having difficulty."

"You're not? But you know I've seen you make this tea many times. I must look completely incompetent to you."

"I know you have been around when I have made tea before, but think back on those times. What were you thinking and doing? I doubt you were sitting there intensely studying my process."

Kamia thought back and admitted to Tuta that she was not really paying attention to all the steps in the recipe. She was just sitting back and waiting for the tea to be served to her.

"Yes. You see, just like everything else in life, my love, making my special tea is a learned skill. It does not come naturally. It must be taught to someone when she or he is making a conscious effort to learn."

Tuta moved over to the counter and began assembling all the ingredients for her tea. She carefully grated the ginger and juiced the lemon. Then, she steeped the tea for exactly five minutes. Once the tea leaves were removed, the grandmother added all the ingredients including what appeared to be a half teaspoon each of honey and cinnamon and then stirred the mixture vigorously to blend all the flavours and allow the tea to cool slightly. Kamia watched intently as she had never done before. Although Tuta measured the ingredients by eye, Kamia could still get a good sense of how much of each ingredient was used. When she could see that the tea was nearly ready, Kamia got two tall glasses from her cupboard and filled them with ice. Tuta poured the warm tea over the ice and added a slice of lemon and a mint leaf to each glass. Mint! Of course! Thought Kamia. How could she have forgotten the mint?!

"There you go my dear," said Tuta gently as she handed her granddaughter a glass of tea. "That wasn't so hard, was it?"

"No," said Kamia ashamed of herself. "I'm sorry Tuta, I should have..."

"Nonsense my dear," interrupted the grandmother. "This exercise was not designed to make you look bad, but to demonstrate that, even with all the will in the world—which I truly believe you have by the way—it's almost impossible for someone to do what you're asking of them if they don't really know how to do it."

"But it's just doing dishes and laundry and a little bit of time with their own children. How can that be so hard?"

"Forgive me my dear, but I could say the same thing about the tea. Just because you knew *what* I wanted you to do, did not mean you knew *how* to do it. If I were to show you *how* to make the tea and you were to practice a couple of times, you would become very good at it and you would become more and more comfortable with the task."

"Oh. I guess you're right grandmother." Kamia lowered her eyes in embarrassment.

"Tell me granddaughter, how did you feel when you were trying to make my tea but could not remember how to do it?"

"Uh, worried and maybe even a little afraid."

"Exactly. And that's the same with most people—especially men—when they are faced with doing things they don't really know how to do. And what do you think they might be afraid of?"

"They could be afraid of a lot of things," Kamia answered nervously. "Afraid of failing, afraid of looking stupid."

"Afraid of failing and looking stupid *in front of their wife*," added Tuta emphatically.

Kamia nodded in agreement.

"So faced with a fear of failing and looking stupid, what do you think most men would do?" asked the grandmother.

"Probably avoid whatever the task is. Or become really defensive about it. Or both!"

Kamia laughed, reflecting on the last couple of weeks she had spent frustrated with her husbands.

"Ahhh. Now I think you *see* what I am getting at, Kamia," began Tuta. "Most people are afraid of the things that they haven't done before because it means they have to leave their *comfort zone of the familiar*–the things they already know how to do–the stuff that makes them feel good about themselves. Sometimes when you ask them to do something they don't know how to do they might even think you are setting them up for failure. Or, they might have simply convinced themselves that they will fail."

"That's crazy. They are both smart capable men. They can certainly learn to fold laundry and do dishes. And why would I want them to fail? I need their help! This whole idea is ridiculous!"

"Sometimes people's fear is irrational. Please try to understand, Kamia, that fear doesn't have to make sense to be real. Both your husbands have watched for quite some time now as you care for the house and the children with grace and ease. They have seen how well the children respond to you—how natural you are with them—so it is quite possible that Tom and Allen might be afraid they will never measure up."

Kamia paused for a moment. She'd never thought about it that way before. She'd had years of experience caring for children and a home. Even as a child, and especially after her mother died, she was often involved in looking after younger siblings and completing domestic chores alongside older female relatives. And when she thought back to how she felt when her first child was born, she remembered being afraid of failing and feeling overwhelmed by all the chores that needed to be done. It took some time, practice and guidance from other women for her to develop the confidence she now had interacting with the kids and meeting all their needs. Maybe her husbands were being intimidated by what a good job she does. Maybe they could use some help getting over their fear of failure.

"OK, Tuta. So what if all that is true? They would never admit it. And they certainly would never ask for my help!" declared Kamia.

"Oh my dear you are so right indeed!" Tuta agreed wholeheartedly. "The prideful nature of men does get in the way here, there can be no doubt!" The two women laughed knowingly for a moment before the grandmother continued.

"Your challenge is to help your husbands get past whatever fears they might have and then gently give them specific direction on how to do the things you need them to do. Remember, they are men, they want to please you and especially to feel successful. They might just need some additional direction and instruction on *exactly how to do what you need them to do.*"

"Thank you Tuta. Such wonderful advice, yet again. I am a very lucky girl to have such a wise grandmother to help me."

"Oh! And one more thing, Kamia," interjected Tuta. "As you teach them *how* to do what you want them to do, be sure that you are *guiding them,* not bossing them around. Men hate that, as I am sure you know, my dear." Kamia smiled heartily and nodded in agreement. Tuta would get no argument there.

The two women spent the next hour chatting about friends and family and then Tuta went home.

That evening, Kamia reflected on her conversation with her grandmother. Now that she thought about it, it did seem quite likely that her two husbands really didn't know how to do some of the things she had asked them to do. Just like she didn't really know how to make her Tuta's famous tea. Thanks to her grandmother's latest installment of excellent advice, she knew what she had to do.

The next night after the children were in bed asleep, Kamia asked both her husbands to join her once again in the living room for a chat.

"Guys," Kamia began, "First of all, I want you to know that I really appreciate all that you two have been trying to do these past couple of weeks. I really appreciate it. But, I think you would agree, we're having problems with some of the chores we've been trying to get done." Kamia spoke very carefully. She used the word "we" on purpose so as to avoid any suggestion of blame. Kamia knew it was critical to honour her husbands' egos and avoid any direct criticism.

"Oh, no!" cried Allen. "Not this again. What's wrong now? You know that I've been trying."

Kamia was starting to worry that her husbands weren't listening to what she had just said and were going to quickly become tense and defensive.

"Yeah," Tom joined in, "Me too! As a matter of fact, I'm starting to drive myself crazy with it. Look at my dishpan hands!"

The three of them laughed. Kamia was thankful for the comic relief.

"Relax guys," Kamia said. "Like I just said, I'm here to tell you that I know you've been trying. But I also want to ask you one thing."

"What's that?" the two husbands blurted out simultaneously.

"I want to know if you *know how to do* what I am asking you to do?"

"What? You think we're idiots or something?" Allen blurted out. "Did you hear that Tom? She doesn't think we know how to load the dishwasher and bathe our own kids!"

"Yeah, Kamia," began Tom. "Come on, we aren't totally morons."

"Wait guys, that's not what I meant at all!" Kamia exclaimed. She was starting to get nervous now. "Why are they being so defensive?" she thought to herself. Then she remembered what Tuta had been saying about men fearing failure so she quickly tried to explain herself.

"Please don't get upset. Just hear me out. It's not just you! It's me too. You both know how everyone loves Tuta's tea. Well, yesterday, she came over and at one point she asked me to make it for her. But here's the crazy part. I couldn't. At least not the way she would make it!" She stumbled to get her point across but it wasn't working.

"OK Kamia, what are you talking about?" asked Tom. "What on earth does tea have to do with us being too stupid to do basic chores and babysitting?"

"No! That's the whole point. It's not about you guys being stupid. Just like with the tea. I was trying to make it myself, but I couldn't remember all the steps and ingredients even though I had watched Tuta make it hundreds of times. You see I felt stupid then, but really, it was just that I had never really known how to make it. She did it in front of me so many times, but I never really thought about it enough to learn *how* to do it myself. She just made it look so simple that I figured I should have just been able to do it on my own. But I couldn't because I didn't really know how until she taught me directly."

"So you're saying you know how to do all this stuff around the house because you learned it somewhere?" asked Allen. "Like from your mother or your aunts? But we were never really involved in that kind of stuff as kids."

"Yeah, my mother did everything for me." Tom laughed. "I never had to lift a finger around the house."

"Must be nice you lazy doofus!" teased Allen. "I had chores to do as a kid. But now that I think of it, they were mostly outside with my dads."

"Yeah me too," said Tom. "I guess all those inside things were happening all around us, but we never paid much attention to any of it."

"See, there you go!" Kamia spoke up again. "It's not about being stupid, it's about not having enough experience doing something that seems simple on the surface, but does require a bit of instruction. I've been doing this kind of work since I was a little kid. If you'll just let me spend a bit of time with you guys showing you a few strategies that I've learned on how to do those inside jobs, I know you'll have no trouble getting the hang of it." Kamia could see that her husbands faces were starting to soften. They looked at each other for a moment and then Allen spoke up.

"OK. Sure. Maybe that's a good idea. It might make it a bit easier for us. I mean, sometimes I do wonder if I'm doing things the right way, or at least the way you want me to do them. For what it's worth, I guess I always told myself that you'd tell me if I was doing it wrong. But maybe I should have asked you."

"What about you, Tom?" Allen asked.

"Well," came his reply. "I sort of feel the same way. I know what you want me to do, Kami, but I'm just not always sure that I can do it in a way that will make you satisfied and happy. I don't feel very confident, I guess."

"Great." said Kamia. "So I want to take those worries away—for the both of you. I've finally realized that I need to help show you *how* to do what I need you to do."

Kamia then suggested to the men that perhaps she could work alongside them over the next week or two to help them with some of the household tricks she had learned over the years. She explained that she didn't want to take over or micromanage them, but rather support what they were doing with some help and advice. Just so they better understood how to do the things she wanted them to do.

Both husbands agreed to accept Kamia's help.

Kamia went to bed that night feeling a renewed sense of hope and confidence.

Chapter 3

The Third Question: Does he know *why* he should do it?

The two weeks of Kamia helping Tom and Allen learn how to do their jobs went well. Tom was especially keen and excited about having to spend more time with the kids. Allen, on the other hand, was attentive but not quite as enthusiastic as Tom. Overall, though, both men seemed to find their stride after a few sessions of help from Kamia. At that point, she felt comfortable stepping back and letting the men take over on their own.

For the first couple of weeks after that, things went remarkably well. Both husbands remembered what to do and did it with few gentle reminders from Kamia. She was starting to feel very proud of herself. Finally, her husbands were pitching in and she had some time to breathe, some time just for herself.

Slowly over time unfortunately, Kamia noticed a deterioration in the men's commitment. There were two nights in a row that Allen wasn't home until 9pm so Kamia ended up having to help Tom out with the kitchen and the kids. It was clear from Tom's attitude that he was not impressed that he had to do chores when Allen didn't. That Saturday, Tom went out to play tennis all day leaving Allen to do the laundry on his own. Tom thought it served Allen right after he had missed two evenings worth of dishes and baths. However, while there were many clothes to wash, Allen only did one load of laundry that weekend consisting mostly of his own clothes.

Soon after, with tensions mounting in the family, things really started going downhill. Allen continued his spotty attendance in the evenings and slacked-off on weekends. Tom continued to disappear on Saturdays. The children started complaining to Kamia again that their dads weren't always reading them their bedtime stories. Throughout it all, Kamia promised herself that she would maintain her composure and gentle up-beat demeanor hoping things would correct themselves. But they did not.

Kamia couldn't understand how this could be happening. Everything had been going so well for the first while. She had no doubt that Tom and Allen knew *what* she wanted them to do and *how* they were supposed to be doing it. So why was everything falling apart? Kamia was at her wits' end.

She thought again about how well her grandmother's husbands seemed to happily go about fulfilling Tuta's needs and she became ashamed of herself. She knew she must be doing something wrong, but what could it be? She had followed all her grandmother's advice but still wasn't getting what she needed from her husbands.

Kamia knew she was going to see Tuta the next day at a family picnic, but she was not looking forward to it. She normally loved to spend time with her grandmother, but now she was dreading it. Tuta would surely be asking how things with her husbands were going and she was embarrassed to tell her the truth. Her grandmother had already given Kamia a lot of her time. By now she must be wondering what on earth was the matter with her granddaughter.

Kamia sensed there was something she was missing—something that would bring it all together. She just didn't know what it was. It was either go back to Tuta in the hope that she could supply the missing link or just give up. But Kamia was not a giving-up kind of woman. So the next day at the picnic, she found her grandmother sitting alone in a chair under a large oak tree quietly enjoying the fresh air. She went over to Tuta figuring she might as well take the bull by the horns and ask for more advice right away.

As soon as Kamia began to approach, the old woman's face lit up and she called out: "How wonderful to see you, my dear! How are the children?" Kamia thought it was kind of her grandmother not to jump right to the trouble with her marriages.

"Hello grandmother." Kamia kissed her on the cheek. "The children are doing well, thank you for asking. How are you?"

"Oh, you know, these old bones creak a bit, but my mind is still sharp as a tack!" The old woman pointed to her head and laughed out loud.

Kamia hardly broke a smile. Tuta could tell there was something wrong so she asked gently: "What is it dear? You seem unhappy."

"I am so very unhappy Tuta," Kamia began. "I feel ridiculous having to come back to you yet again. I mean, I know how much you've already helped me and..."

"Passing on wisdom to young people is what grandmothers are for, dear. Tell me what is going on."

"Well," began Kamia. "I tried everything you suggested with Tom and Allen and it seemed like it was working at first, but now it's all come apart again. I feel so ashamed that I am here recounting another failure to you, grandmother. After all the help you've given me, I still can't seem to get my husbands to do what I need them to do." Tears began to well up in the young woman's eyes.

"Now, now, granddaughter. Chin up," said Tuta. "It is to your credit that you seek out help when you need it. Heavens, I wasn't born knowing how to manage my marriages, you know. I had help when I first started out. And I've had many years to make mistakes and learn from them. If I can help you avoid a few, I'm delighted to do so. And then, when you've had some experience, I hope you'll help your own granddaughter one day."

Kamia breathed a sigh of relief. Once again she was reminded why she admired her grandmother so much. "I'm still struggling with Tom and Allen. I did everything you said, and then they started to get better but now they have gone back to their old ways."

"Are you certain they both know *what* to do?" asked Tuta.

"Undeniably," Kamia responded. "They know what they agreed to do and they understand what specifically needs to be done for each task. I know this for sure."

"And do they know *how* to do the tasks they have agreed to?"

"Without a doubt," came the response from the young woman. "They both spent time with me where I showed them how to do all the tasks and then I watched as they did each task on their own. They asked many questions and I answered them all. And for the first couple of weeks everything seemed to go very well."

"I see," said the wise old woman. "But do they know *why* they should do these things you ask of them?"

"Do they know *why* they should be doing these things?" repeated Kamia with an incredulous tone in her voice. "I should certainly hope so."

"Well, you better make sure because when men don't understand the point of doing something–the *why* of what they are doing–they tend to put that thing on the back burner in favour of those tasks that seem to make more sense to them, that seem to have more of a purpose. If Tom and Allen don't understand the *why*, it will be a lot harder for them to make time in their busy day for the things you want them to do. So if I were you, I would make sure that they both know *why* they need to do what they agreed to do."

At first it seemed so obvious to Kamia why her husbands should do what she wanted them to do. They said they would, after all. She needed help and, as their wife, they should help her. Isn't that *why* enough? Kamia was getting frustrated.

"But Tuta," Kamia pleaded, "I already used that argument with them before and it didn't seem to make a difference. So what should I do now?"

"I see," said the wise old lady. "However, did you explain *why* they should be doing things in a way that a man can understand. Sometimes ideas that seem obvious to women often need special branding to resonate with men," explained Tuta. "Let me tell you a little story that I often use to help my husbands understand *why* they need to do something I have asked for."

Tuta told Kamia the story and the young woman knew right away she could use it with her husbands. Just as Tuta finished, some of her great-grandchildren interrupted to drag her off to play with them. Kamia was left to reflect on Tuta's latest words of wisdom.

After dinner the next night, while the kids were off playing, Kamia and her husbands sat at the dining room table lingering over a glass of wine and a special dessert Tom had brought home that evening. Kamia began casually telling the story her grandmother had recommended.

"So my darling husbands, I just saw this really interesting documentary about these migratory birds in North America," she began. "There are really big heavy birds called Canada Geese that fly something like 8,000 miles round trip each and every year! In the fall, they travel from their home in Canada to spend the winter in Mexico, and then return back to Canada in the spring. It's an incredible journey. Many scientists have speculated as to what could possibly enable such birds— birds that look 'aerodynamically challenged'—to accomplish such a feat. It is generally believed that it has a lot to do with how they fly together in this 'V' formation." Kamia made a sideways "V" shape with her arms and hands as she spoke.

"Hey yeah! I saw some birds like that last time I was in Hawaii," added Tom. "I think they were called Golden Plovers. But same deal, they flew in a 'V' too." Tom made the same shape with his arms too and both Kamia and Allen laughed.

"That's very interesting," said Allen showing little enthusiasm for the topic. "So, what's the point?"

Kamia saw that as a chance to jump back in and finish her story.

"You see, the lead bird, the one at the tip of the 'V' has the primary responsibility for setting the direction for the flock and for navigation. The only problem is that the lead bird takes the full brunt of the wind's force and tires very quickly."

"Well that doesn't seem fair," interjected Allen. "Why should he have to be the one who works the hardest?"

"Actually," Kamia went on "When the lead bird gets tired, a special maneuver takes place in which the lead bird rotates to the back of the flock's 'V' formation and the next bird in line takes over flying at the tip. I think they called it the 'flying point'."

With the men listening intently, Kamia continued talking.

"Scientists believe that as each bird flaps its huge wings, it creates a minor up-draft, or up-lift, for the birds following behind. And the effect is cumulative. So, the strongest uplift from all the birds flapping their wings is felt at the very back—which just happens to be the place where the bird that is most tired goes to recuperate after having flown in front at the tip."

"Huh, that's really interesting," Tom said sincerely. "So it's totally fair, then. Everybody helps and everybody benefits."

Kamia started to get a little excited as she noticed Tom engaging in the story. "That's right. But the key to the birds' success lies in the fact that each bird knows what it must do to help the whole flock accomplish its mission. Each bird knows and understands the importance of staying in formation and each bird knows the important role that it plays—whatever its position—in terms of helping the entire flock achieve its goals both more effectively and efficiently. So none of the birds is saying to himself, 'What I do doesn't matter.' It doesn't say, 'No one really cares whether I stay in formation or not.' Instead, it knows that what it does—no matter how small it may seem to be—contributes to the success of the flock and that if it were to break formation, it could jeopardize the entire group."

"OK, I get it," said Allen rolling his eyes. "You're telling us about these birds because you want us to see how important everyone's effort is to the success of our family, right?"

"Actually, I hadn't thought of that," she smiled coyly. "But now that you mention it, the story does fit. We all have a vital and important role to play in keeping things running smoothly so that everyone's needs are met and we all feel appreciated and satisfied. Without everyone's full participation, we can't expect the kids to be properly cared for, the house to be kept properly clean and our relationships to be joyful, healthy and peaceful."

"I guess that's really true everywhere," said Tom. "At work, playing sports, things always go more smoothly when everyone does their part and remembers why what they do matters."

Allen nodded in reluctant agreement. "Yeah, everything sure slows down at the office when one or two people aren't working with effort and enthusiasm. I've seen that situation ruin more than one deal."

"That's cool, Kamia, I never really thought about our family that way before," said Tom.

"That's OK," said Kamia. "I'm just sorry that we didn't have this conversation earlier. It might have made things a lot easier in terms of knowing *why* I was doing some of the things that I did and knowing *why* I needed you to do certain things in a certain way. I'm sorry for not explaining it better."

"But you should also know," continued Kamia. "I really do value what you and Allen are doing and I continue to need your help if we are going to become a successful family. It's comforting to know that I can count on you, both."

"You can count on us. Right, Allen?" said Tom.

"Sure," responded Allen.

Chapter 4

The Fourth Question:
Does he know he
should care?

After that conversation with her husbands, Kamia felt confident moving forward. She felt like the two men really understood why they needed to be more attentive husbands and fathers. She felt she could focus more on her own life and personal priorities and she did relax more as things at home seemed to develop a natural rhythm. As proof, one night Tom mentioned to Kamia in bed how much fun he was having in the evenings during bath and story time. He told her it was becoming his favourite part of the day.

"I never realized that taking care of our kids could be this entertaining," said Tom. "It's really inspiring me to come up with new jokes and games to make them laugh."

Kamia also started to notice how the kids would light-up on nights when it was Tom's turn to put them to bed and how they would slump down a little in their chairs at dinner when they found out Allen would be in charge that night.

For some reason, Allen just wasn't getting with the program. While he was still apparently trying to make a contribution, he still complained a lot about the housework he had to do and Kamia rarely heard the children laughing when Allen was in charge of bedtime. Worse, Allen continued to come home late and avoid his evening responsibilities leaving her to pick up the slack.

It's not that Tom was perfect or anything. While he was great at putting the kids to bed, he sometimes complained about doing the dishes and often did a sloppy job with the laundry. But that was still an improvement over Allen who often "forgot" to do his chores all together. He just really seemed to be stuck in his old ways.

In mulling over the situation in her mind, Kamia reached the conclusion that both Allen and Tom certainly had to know *why* they needed to do what they had agreed to do but, for some reason, they were still not doing everything she needed them to do.

She decided to speak to Tuta yet once again.

"Do they know *what* to do?" the wise old woman asked patiently.

"Yes," Kamia replied.

"And do they know *how* to do it?"

"Definitely."

"And do they know *why* they should do it?"

"Unquestionably," came the response. "Tuta, we've been through all of it together and they both know they can come to me for help if they need it."

"I see," said Tuta, "But do they know that they should *care* about doing it?"

"Do they know they should *care*?" asked an exasperated Kamia. "How could they *not* know they should care? Plus, I have held their hands through every detail. What more can I do?"

"Well for starters dear," began the grandmother, "You can make sure they know you are paying attention to how well they are doing."

"But, but..." sputtered Kamia, "I already do that. Whenever they miss something or do something wrong, I always tell them—very gently, I might add—how unhappy it makes me that they are not living up to their promises."

"But doing so, even gently, can make them defensive," observed Tuta. "Isn't that right, dear?"

"Well, now that you say that, as a matter of fact, it usually does. They often get upset—sometimes quite upset—when I point out their mistakes. But I'm the one who should be upset. I'm the one who is left to do extra work," stated Kamia indignantly. "I don't get why they think it's OK for *them* to get angry. I should be the one getting angry!"

"I see," said Tuta. Then she paused and sighed. "So you scold your prideful husbands like children and then you wonder why they get upset. It sounds to me like you are not really behaving as a loving partner with them. You are acting more like a policeman hiding in the bushes waiting to hand out speeding tickets."

Kamia was very surprised to hear her grand-mother's response. She didn't know what to say, so she sat there in silence.

"Kamia, let me ask you something. Apart from your criticism after the men have failed to meet your expectations, how do Tom and Allen know if they are doing a good a job or not? How do they know when they are doing things well so they can keep on doing them that way?"

Tuta paused to wait for an answer.

"Um, I'm not really too sure," offered Kamia.

"And when you are scolding them, do you point out what they have done well? And do you provide specific feedback to help them improve?

"I'm not sure, Tuta. Usually, I'm usually so frustrated at the time that I doubt I offer any compliments. And I can't really remember how specific my criticism is. I suppose I just rely on Tom and Allen to figure out what they did wrong."

"My dear, so many young wives make the same mistake–as I too did once. By now, your husbands already know that they need to improve. But, it's often hard for them to measure how well they're doing what you need them to do, especially when they are in the thick of things. Imagine a competitive sport, Kamia, in which no one on the team–and no one in the audience watching–knows the score of a game until the very end, or until the referee simply decides to tell everyone. It would be very hard to play, not much fun to watch and it would make it difficult deciding when to cheer or change strategy. So you need some kind process that lets the players and the referees know the score as the game proceeds."

Tuta went on. "Now the same holds true for Tom and Allen. They need to know on a regular and consistent basis how well they are doing. And not just how they are doing in a particular moment, but how well they are progressing overall. That way they can react in a more timely way and not after it's too late to do anything about it—when the game is almost over."

"Oh, OK. I think I understand now," began Kamia. "All that negative feedback after they have failed is kinda demoralizing for them. I guess it might even make them feel like they don't want to bother trying anymore."

"Indeed, my clever granddaughter. You're catching on now," said Tuta encouragingly. "In particular, you need to praise them when they are doing things well. Most normal men actively seek to please a woman they believe *can be pleased.* And if they really believe you are happy with them, they will want to continue their efforts."

"I see. And so, if I do what you've just told me," said Kamia, "Will Tom and Allen start to *care* about what I need them to do?"

"Not necessarily," answered Tuta.

"What do you mean, 'not necessarily'?" exclaimed Kamia, somewhat horrified.

"I mean that sometimes the feedback you give isn't always enough to motivate a husband to really *care*–to do what you need him to do. And that's because there is still another reason why they might not care."

With Kamia's encouragement, the wise old woman continued.

"It has to do with consequences, my dear. For some people, if there are no personal consequences associated with doing, or not doing certain things, they will not be as committed to doing them as they might otherwise be. So when this happens to any of your husbands, you have to figure out a way to let them know that what they choose to do–or not do–really matters, and that it matters to them *personally* in a way that men understand."

"What kind of consequences, Tuta. Are you talking about...in the bedroom?" said Kamia hesitantly.

"Yes, and no," answered the grandmother with a sly grin growing on her face. "There is no doubt that sex can be a powerful motivator for men. But there are also other ways to really motivate men with *positive* consequences. And the ones that I have found to be the most useful are *recognition* and *admiration*–you know, the private and public praising of a man that shows how much he is valued, appreciated and loved by his wife and family."

"OK, so what I need to do is to tell them when they are doing a good job. That's easy enough," said Kamia.

"Well that is certainly part of it, but you need to do more than that. Men thrive on admiration and appreciation. They crave it from their wives but it is even more powerful when it is received publicly. Men want others to know they are valued too."

Kamia reflected on what her grandmother had just said. Now that she thought about it, she did remember hearing Tuta speak very positively about her husbands many, many times. But she had to admit that she could not remember a single time that she had ever even complimented Tom or Allen in public. She just expected them to be good husbands without needing to praise them for it.

"I hadn't really thought about it like that before, Tuta," said Kamia. "Once again, you have given me really good advice. But why didn't you tell me about this 'caring' stuff when I first came to see you to talk about my problems with Tom and Allen?"

"Well, my dear, the difficulties you described with your marriages often simply disappear once most husbands know *what* to do, *how* to do it, and *why* they should do it."

"Oh."

"When most men know the *what*, the *why* and the *how* of their roles as husbands and fathers, they will usually do what you ask them to do because you've helped them feel competent and confident in doing it. In other words, they feel good about themselves as husbands. And they feel good about themselves because they know that what they are doing counts, that it makes a difference, and they can see the role that they have to play in helping the whole family succeed. Sometimes, once all these pieces are in place, they will find their own motivation to do what they need to do."

"Come to think of it," Kamia interrupted, "Tom does really seem to enjoy his time at night with the kids. And he's a superstar getting stubborn stains out of clothes."

"How wonderful!" cried the old woman joyfully. "However, when you find yourself at a point where the *what*, the *how* and the *why* are all in place and you're still not getting everything you want and need as a wife, you should not despair. Your efforts haven't been wasted. That's because you need to have the *what*, the *how* and the *why* in place first before you can start setting up processes to help your husbands realize that they should *care*. If you haven't done so already along the way. Otherwise, you are just setting them up to fail."

"Oh dear."

"Yes, my granddaughter." Tuta paused. "Think about it. How would you like to have a job to do that was supposed to be rewarding and fulfilling, but you didn't understand exactly *what* it was that you needed to do? Or how would you like to know that if you fail in your role that there would be negative consequences but you didn't really understand *how* to succeed? And no one would show you? A wise wife has to make sure that all her husbands know the *what*, the *how* and the *why* first. Only when these are in place, and there are still problems, can she begin to help them understand why they should *care*."

Just then Tuta's fourth husband walked in to let her know that dinner was ready.

"Would you like to join us, Kamia?"

"No thank you, Tuta. I must get back to my family now. You have given me so much to think about and you have been so generous with your time and advice. Goodnight." And with that, Kamia kissed her grandmother and left to go home and contemplate everything the wise old woman had just told her.

***

Several days passed as Kamia thought through her plans to help Allen and Tom care about what they were doing. However, her thinking was interrupted by some encouraging developments. One night when Allen had stayed late at work, despite the fact that it was his turn to do the dishes, Tom got up from the table and just began cleaning up on his own. No complaints about having to pick up the slack for Allen. Nothing. He just cleaned up the kitchen quietly. He did forget to run the dishwasher, but still, Kamia was pleased.

Kamia, for the first time, was beginning to feel a sense of accomplishment for the work she was doing—insofar as Tom was concerned, anyway. It was significant to her that Tom took over Allen's household chores that night. She was quick to thank him and praise him with loving words and a hug for his willingness to step-up.

With Allen, however, the lack of progress was still very upsetting. He continued to skip out on chores and only half-heartedly engaged with the kids. It must have been obvious to Allen that the children preferred bedtime with Tom, but that didn't seem to bother him. He was simply not living up to his responsibilities and not engaging with the family.

A few days later, Kamia felt she was finally ready with a plan that would hopefully get both Allen and Tom caring more about their roles in the family. Remembering Tuta's advice once again, she was prepared to give her husbands the benefit of the doubt. It was quite possible that she was too focused on the negative. Maybe she was looking too hard for failure and not being open to celebrating her husbands' successes. Afterall, both men had made progress over where they had been six months ago. She did not want to find herself becoming one of those wives who is never satisfied with her husbands' efforts no matter how much they do.

Kamia decided to chat separately with each husband this time. She started with Tom, since she knew he would be the most receptive. So, one night when Allen was working late, Kamia decided to help Tom with the dishes.

"Hey, I got this," said Tom.

"Thanks, honey. But I'd like to help," insisted Kamia.

As they worked together, Kamia casually opened the conversation about caring.

"You know, Tom. I've really noticed how you have been working hard around here lately to support me and the kids."

"Yeah, I have been trying pretty hard. Thanks for noticing," he said as he nudged her playfully with his elbow.

"Do you feel like I haven't really been noticing enough, you know, how you've been doing?" asked Kamia.

"Well, to be perfectly honest, you really don't say too much about what I do around here, unless you're complaining."

Kamia paused to think for a moment.

"Yeah, I guess you're right," she said. "I do complain when I'm unhappy about stuff."

"But Kami, to be fair, you usually wait until you're really frustrated, so then you get cranky about it," began Tom. "I'm going along thinking everything is just fine and then you get mad that I've been missing something. It would be much better if you just told me about stuff nicely–and right away–without all that tension in your voice or waiting until bedtime or the next day."

"OK," said Kamia, a little stunned. "Thank you for telling me that. I guess that behaviour on my part would make you feel pretty defensive."

Tom laughed out loud. "You think?" he said sarcastically and then they both chuckled about it together.

"Well, honey, for the record, you are doing really well. And I want you to know that I really appreciate how much effort you are putting in," Kamia said, pausing for a moment. "In the spirit of our chat tonight, I would say one other thing. Maybe you could try to be a bit more careful folding the laundry?"

"Sure," began Tom with a smile. "Yeah, I guess I do struggle with folding. Maybe you could help me with a little refresher course this weekend."

Kamia smiled back in agreement. After a moment of silence, Tom hesitantly offered up a question. "So, how do you think it's going with the kids? You know, the night time bath and bed routine?"

Kamia was surprised to hear Tom ask this question. It was very obvious to her that this part of the process had been going extremely well. How could he not see that too?

"That part has been awesome, baby," she said and kissed him on the lips. "The kids have told me how much they love their evenings with you and I can tell just by listening to all the laughter that it's going great." She paused and then added, "But hey, I thought you knew that already."

"Well, yeah, I guess I thought it was going pretty well, but you never know. It's nice to hear you say it. So thanks. I'm glad the kids are having fun. I am too." Allen continued, "Hearing you say that really helps me feel more confident—that I'm headed down the right road."

Once again Kamia marveled at how right her grandmother had been. She was definitely not giving Tom enough regular positive feedback on how well he was doing.

"I'm going to work harder to make sure I give you more positive feedback, Tom," Kamia began. "I feel badly that I wasn't doing more of that before."

"That's OK, honey," said Tom. "I appreciate that you're telling me now. And I'm really glad that you are going to help with the folding this weekend." They looked at each other and smiled and then Tom leaned in to hug Kamia lovingly.

Later that night, while she was working in her office, Kamia could not stop thinking about how well her conversation with Tom had gone. She felt a renewed sense of hope and confidence and was now looking forward to having the same chat with Allen.

***

The next day, Kamia found Allen sitting outside on the porch in the evening after the children had gone to bed. She thought this might be a good time to talk with him as she had with Tom the day before.

Because things had gone so well with Tom, Kamia began with Allen in much the same way. She sat down and told her husband, with a loving tone in her voice, that she wanted him to know she had noticed all his positive efforts around the house. Unfortunately, Allen became irritated almost im-mediately.

"Geez Kamia, I don't need a pep talk from you. I'm already doing the best I can," Allen said.

"Hey baby, I only meant to let you know that I really appreciate your efforts."

"Oh, OK. Thanks," Allen replied curtly.

After a moment, Kamia continued. "So honey, lately I've been thinking that maybe I don't talk to you enough about how you're doing with everything, especially the good stuff."

"Look, Kamia, you always complain when everything isn't perfect. And I really feel deep inside that whatever I do will never be good enough for you. So I get nervous when you want to talk about how it's going. I guess I just expect more criticism."

"Well, that's kind of my point Allen. And I'm sorry that I have made you feel that way. I don't want to be critical all the time. I want to show you my appreciation more often when things are going well. And offer reminders more gently when I need to. I don't want to be getting all cranky about things. I love you."

"I don't need any reminders," Allen shot back. "I'm already doing everything I can."

"But honey, you still come home late sometimes and leave it to me or Tom to clean up the kitchen," said Kamia in a gentle, non-confrontational voice.

"What? That hardly ever happens," shouted Allen, clearly angry now. "I'm there most nights when I'm supposed to be. And when I can't, it's because I have to work. You know how demanding my job is."

"Baby, we all have demanding jobs. But Tom and I still manage to take care of things at home too."

"So what are you saying?" asked Allen aggressively "You're not happy that I am devoted to my work?"

"No that's not it, I'm just saying..."

"You know what, Kam? I really don't understand why it's such a big deal," interrupted Allen. "When I'm home, I always do what you want. Why can't you help me out with the dishes and the kids now and then when I can't get away from the office?"

"OK honey. I'm not trying to upset you. And you're right. I guess it's not that big a deal now and then. But what about on the weekends? You haven't done any laundry in a month."

Allen rolled his eyes. "OK fine. I'll try to do better there."

At this point Kamia was too afraid to mention bedtime and bath time. So she tried to focus on the housekeeping tasks.

"That's great. Thanks honey," she began. "Is there anything I can do to help you? Anything you are having trouble with?"

"No, I'm fine. I told you that I'll do better."

Allen then got up and went back into the house. Kamia did not follow him. She sat out on the deck feeling disappointed that her conversation with Allen had not gone as well as she had hoped. She felt discouraged, but decided to let some time pass to see if things would improve.

***

As the weeks passed, it was clear that Tuta had been right again–at least as far as Tom was concerned.

After Kamia had given Tom a bit more help with the laundry, his attitude and folding skills improved greatly. He even came up with the idea to get the kids to help put the clothes away after they had been folded. Kamia was happy to see the kids taking on some responsibility and Tom made a game of it with them so they all seemed to be having fun too.

Even more impressive was the fact that Tom started using a lot of Kamia's strategies when he was managing the kids. Whether he was breaking up a fight or trying to get the kids to do something, Tom was taking them through the *what, how, why* and *caring* concepts–and it was working with them too. It turns out that this approach can even help children come to achieve their potential more easily and with little or no push-back.

Remembering Tuta's advice, Kamia started to make a point of telling the kids how lucky they were to have such a great dad as Tom. She also began to express her admiration for Tom when they were out with friends and family. To her delight, her public compliments would always make him beam with pride.

Tom was working hard which made Kamia feel supported, and as a result, closer to him. As Tom was becoming more and more invested in family life, Kamia found herself looking forward to her nights alone with him. Their love-making had become more romantic and fun in the last little while which she knew he enjoyed as much as she did. Kamia began to understand what Tuta had alluded to earlier about sex being a powerful reward for men. It wasn't that she was using sex to motivate Tom, it was just that as he worked harder to be fully engaged with the family, their sex-life had naturally improved.

Unfortunately, things were not going so well with Allen. Since their uncomfortable exchange on the porch, Allen seemed to have become even more withdrawn. He continued to avoid household chores and his engagement with the children did not improve either. It was almost like he wasn't even trying.

Kamia's frustration and growing resentment over Allen's lack of effort could not help but spill over into the bedroom. On her nights with Allen she felt the mood was forced and sometimes they would just go to sleep without even saying goodnight. Feeling like she had nothing left to lose, Kamia confronted Allen again.

"Allen, I've tried to be patient, but you just can't seem to give more than a half-hearted effort around here. You seem to view all your responsibilities at home as some kind of burden. Even spending time with the kids doesn't seem to give you any pleasure."

"Not this again, Kamia. Haven't we been through this enough already? I just don't like doing chores. I never had to do them as a kid and I don't want to do them now. OK?"

"No, Allen, it's not OK," replied Kamia with a hint of impatience in her voice. "There are lots of things that we don't like to do in life but still have to do them. So think of the laundry and dishes as some of those things." Kamia's voice became more pleading. "Look, Allen, I really need you to try to do better. The kids need you to try to do better too. They love you and need your attention."

Allen was silent.

Kamia continued. "Is there more I can do to help you? Or maybe you could talk to Tom. He's been doing really well and he might have some tips for you."

"No! I do not need any advice from Tom. I know what I have to do, I just have trouble getting my mind around doing it," Allen shouted.

"Well then, please know that the kids and I really need you to do it. Tom's been able to and it looks bad on you if you don't as well. So, Allen, please try! If not for you, then for us. I know you can do it if you really *care*."

But despite her pleading, things did not get much better. Kamia was running out of ideas with Allen. As Tom continued to be more and more supportive and engaged with Kamia and the kids, Allen became less committed to doing his part. Kamia continued to encourage Allen with positive feedback and she even made additional efforts to spice up their sex-life, but none of it seemed to matter to him.

It was becoming clearer and clearer that both Tom's progress and Allen's lack of interest in change were being reflected in the general tone of their family life. Kamia,

Tom and the kids were having more fun together than ever while Allen started to get short-tempered with everyone and seemed to work late even more than before.

So while Kamia was delighted with the progress that she had made in helping Tom finally do what she needed him to do, she was very disappointed that her efforts with Allen seemed to have fallen flat. She could not explain the differences in outcomes that she had achieved. "I've done everything that Tuta told me to do," she thought to herself. "But I've only managed to succeed with Tom and not with Allen."

Kamia promised herself that she would take the next available opportunity to meet with Tuta and find out what additional wisdom her wise old grand-mother could offer her.

Chapter 5

The Final Question: What if he just ***doesn't get it?***

As Kamia explained the situation to her grandmother, Tuta listened patiently. When Kamia was finished, Tuta repeated her usual litany of questions. Only this time the focus was exclusively on Allen.

"Does he know *what* to do?" came Tuta's traditional opening remark.

"Of course he does, grandmother," answered Kamia.

"And, does he know *how* to do it?" asked Tuta calmly.

"Without question," said Kamia with a hint of frustration growing in her voice.

"And does he know *why* he should do what you want him to do?"

"Yes, he most certainly does," answered Kamia. "Tuta, I've done everything you suggested but..."

101

Tuta continued without missing a beat. "And does he know that he should *care* about doing what you need him to do?"

"Definitely!" replied Kamia, almost shouting now. "Tuta, I've told you all the things that I've done to try and make Allen feel that he should care and still, I'm not getting the behavior or the results that I need from him. What have I done wrong?" Kamia's frustration was now turning into exasperation.

"Well, my clever granddaughter," came Tuta's terse response. "The answer to your question is simple. It's that you haven't done anything wrong. The problem now no longer lies with you to solve. The problem lies with Allen himself—and it appears that he *just doesn't get it!*"

"What do you mean 'he just doesn't get it'?" asked Kamia somewhat confused at Tuta's cryptic words.

"I mean that Allen's personal internal value system and attitudes appear to be so damaged or corrupted that despite your best efforts to show him *what, how, why* and that he *should care,* he is prepared to dig in his heels and defy your best attempts to help assist him. His poor values and attitudes also appear to be so entrenched that it might take you many more months—and maybe even years—to try to reverse them. And unfortunately for

Allen, you probably don't have that amount of time to devote to him, do you?"

"Not really, Tuta," replied Kamia. "I mean, I have a new baby coming soon and the other children and work. I don't see how I can find any more energy to help Allen do what he should be doing anyway."

"Well then, you should probably have a pretty good idea of what it is that you have to do," said Tuta with a sigh. "You see, Kamia, the world is full of people like Allen. Your challenge as a wife is to avoid the 'Allens' you encounter and to find, keep and motivate the 'Toms' that come into your life."

Kamia looked dejected.

"What's wrong my dear?" asked Tuta with concern.

"It's just that I feel badly about Allen. That somehow I failed him."

"You didn't fail Allen. He failed himself." Tuta took a deep breath and continued, "Kamia, you're a talented young woman and a good wife. I admire you greatly. But despite your inexperience, you can't ever allow yourself to forget the most important marriage principle."

"The most important marriage principle? What's that?" asked Kamia.

"It's that when a husband—a partner in your family—isn't doing what it is that needs to be done or not living up to his responsibilities, a caring wife must always commit herself to helping him become the husband she needs." Tuta went on. "When it comes to difficult husbands, wives must ask themselves, 'Do they know *what* to do?', 'Do they know *how* to do it?' 'Do they know *why* they should be doing it?' and 'Do they know that they should *care*?' And if she can answer 'yes' to all four of those questions, then a wife has to accept the fact that somehow an 'Allen' made it into her family—and that he *just doesn't get it*. Only then can she know for sure that she has done everything she can to help him become the man she and her children need. Do you understand that, dear?"

Kamia slowly shook her head yes.

"Of course," continued Tuta, "having married an 'Allen' in the first place, a wife must also consider how to refine her selection process to avoid this mistake in the future. But that is the subject of another whole discussion!" Tuta laughed. "So, go deal with your 'Allen' and start looking for another 'Tom.' Do you see what I'm saying?"

"I think so." replied Kamia.

"Good. Then go forth and prosper, my dear. And remember that you are strong and you will survive this challenge in your life and do better next time."

Kamia thanked her grandmother profusely for all of her patience and help. Kamia sensed somewhat wistfully that her days of running to see the wise old woman were at an end. She knew that Tuta had succeeded in teaching her the most important lessons a wife needs to know.

Kamia promised herself that she would not disappoint her grandmother and that she would master the ways of a great wife as Tuta had helped her understand them.

When Kamia returned to her home, she went to her office to write down what Tuta had taught her:

If wives are unhappy with their husbands, they should remember these 3 things

(1) A good wife always does everything she can to help her husband become the partner she needs him to be.

(2) There are only five reasons why a husband might not do what you need him to do:

• He doesn't know *what* to do.

- He doesn't know **how** to do it.
- He doesn't know **why** he should do it.
- He doesn't know that he **should care**.
- He just **doesn't get it**.

(3) A good wife and partner always makes sure that her husband knows the first four things before she concludes that he "just doesn't get it."

***

A few days later, Kamia went to talk with Allen. They had an open and honest conversation about what Kamia needed Allen to do and what Allen was prepared to give. In light of everything that she had learned from Tuta over the past few months, it came as no surprise to her when Allen himself stated that he was very unhappy and that he wanted a change. It was a relief for both of them to finally put all their cards on the table. Their marriage wasn't working for either of them and it was better to part friends than to allow their relationship to deteriorate any further. Allen was a little disappointed in himself, but he thanked Kamia for all the effort she put into trying to make their marriage work. They both knew it was over.

That night Kamia lay awake with mixed feelings. She had loved Allen, that was certain. But it now seemed as though they simply wanted different things from life and marriage. Kamia knew that it would be difficult for a while adjusting to their separation, but she felt confident that she had done the right thing for her family.

Epilogue

Kamia and Allen quietly divorced. The adults stayed friends throughout the process and they all helped the children adjust to the new family dynamic.

Tom and Kamia continued to grow together. It wasn't long before he was spending more time with the family on weekends as she had wanted. With Kamia's help and support (and Tuta's strategies), Tom also became a much better listener. He was more attentive and knew when she just wanted him to be there for her rather than try to solve all her problems.

Shortly after the baby was born, a new man entered the family as a husband. Kamia had been much more careful when selecting Jim as a new addition. Over the next few years, Kamia married an astonishing five more husbands. While there were certainly some bumps along the road, Kamia consistently used Tuta's philosophy to help guide the men on their journey to becoming wonderful partners in the family.

In time, Kamia became something of a living legend in her community. She was known as the "husband-whisperer" in many circles and was frequently approached for advice by young women in her family. These women would always start out as she did: frustrated, unhappy and bewildered. They would recount their marital troubles to Kamia and when they were through, she would simply smile and say: "I see. So tell me, my dear, does he know *what* to do?"